Frank L. Blanchard

Niagara - the Old and the New

Frank L. Blanchard

Niagara - the Old and the New

ISBN/EAN: 9783743344693

Manufactured in Europe, USA, Canada, Australia, Japa

Cover: Foto ©ninafisch / pixelio.de

Manufactured and distributed by brebook publishing software (www.brebook.com)

Frank L. Blanchard

Niagara - the Old and the New

NIAGARA

THE OLD
AND
THE NEW

LIST OF ILLUSTRATIONS.

TWENTY-RATER NIAGARA.
STEAM YACHT NIAGARA.
THE NIAGARA'S FIGUREHEAD.
GENERAL VIEW OF BRIDGE AND RIGGING.
THE PROMENADE DECK.
OWNER'S OFFICE ON PROMENADE DECK.
TWO VIEWS OF THE MUSIC HALL.
THE CARD ROOM.
LIBRARY AND STAIRCASE.
MRS. GOULD'S SUITE.
MRS. GOULD'S BEDROOM.
BOUDOIR IN MRS. GOULD'S SUITE.
MR. GOULD'S SUITE.
BATHROOM IN MR. GOULD'S SUITE.
DINING-ROOM ON THE MAIN DECK.
ONYX FIREPLACE IN THE DINING-ROOM.
PIANO IN OAK CASE WITH TAPESTRY PANELS.
THE STEWARD'S PANTRY.
GENERAL VIEW OF OWNER'S KITCHEN.
STAIRCASE IN LOWER HALL.

TWENTY-RATER NIAGARA

HE sloop yacht, twenty rater NIAGARA, owned by Mr. Howard Gould, of New York, was built by the Herreshoffs, at Bristol, Rhode Island, in 1895. She is 45 feet long on the water line, 12 feet beam and 10 feet draught.

During the season of 1895 the NIAGARA participated in some fifty races of the leading yacht clubs of Great Britain. Her skipper was John Barr, formerly commander of the Thistle, whose intimate knowledge of the coast and skill in handling her were such that she won twenty-nine first prizes, nine second, and one third prize.

Among the trophies which her owner brought back to New York, as the result of the first summer's work, were the Lord Dunraven Castle Yacht Club Challenge Cup; a silver tea set and tray, presented by Robert Cross for the Royal Western Yacht Club; silver punch bowls from the Clyde, Corinthian, and Royal Albert Yacht Clubs; and silver loving cups from the Royal Western of England and the West of Scotland Yacht Clubs, in addition to the Maitland Kersey Cup, presented by the Castle Yacht Club.

The following year the NIAGARA again competed with English yachts, but her victories were not as numerous as the preceding season, although she won twenty out of forty races in which she participated.

No American yacht ever made such a record in English waters. Her owner was made a life member of the Royal Ulster Yacht Club of Belfast, and an honorary member of the Royal Cork Yacht Club, the Start Bay Yacht Club of Dartmouth, and the Douglas Bay Yacht Club of the Isle of Man.

He was also elected a member of the Royal Largs Yacht Club, the Royal Alfred Yacht Club, and the Royal Temple Yacht Club.

STEAM YACHT NIAGARA

STEAM yacht NIAGARA was launched at the yards of the Harlan & Hollingsworth Co., at Wilmington, Delaware, February 19, 1898, in the presence of a great crowd of people, including a party of invited guests who had come down from New York on a special train. She was christened NIAGARA by Miss Kathrine Clemmons, who subsequently became the wife of Mr. Gould.

The NIAGARA represents the highest type of naval construction as applied to a pleasure craft. She is bark rigged and modelled on lines designed by Captain W. G. Shackford, her commander, late commodore of the Pacific Mail Co.'s fleet.

She was not built for speed, the additional space which extra boilers, furnaces, and coal supply would occupy being devoted to increasing the size of the living rooms and in supplying accommodations not usually found on a yacht.

In point of tonnage the NIAGARA is equalled by only half a dozen yachts in the whole world, her tonnage being 1,445 tons, and her displacement 1,558 tons. She is 272 feet 4 inches long, 36 feet beam, 27 feet 5 inches in depth, and 16 feet 9 inches draught.

She has bilge keels 140 feet in length and 17 inches deep, similar to those employed on the newly built Cunard liners. Capt. Charles G. Lundborg's device is used for protecting the outward shafting of the twin screws.

She has six water-tight steel bulkheads and fore-and-aft bulkheads in the bunkers. The water-tight thwartship bulkheads are of extra strength and thickness. The hull is divided into several independent compartments for additional safety. A water bottom runs the entire length of the ship.

The NIAGARA flies the flag of the New York Yacht Club in addition to the owner's colors.

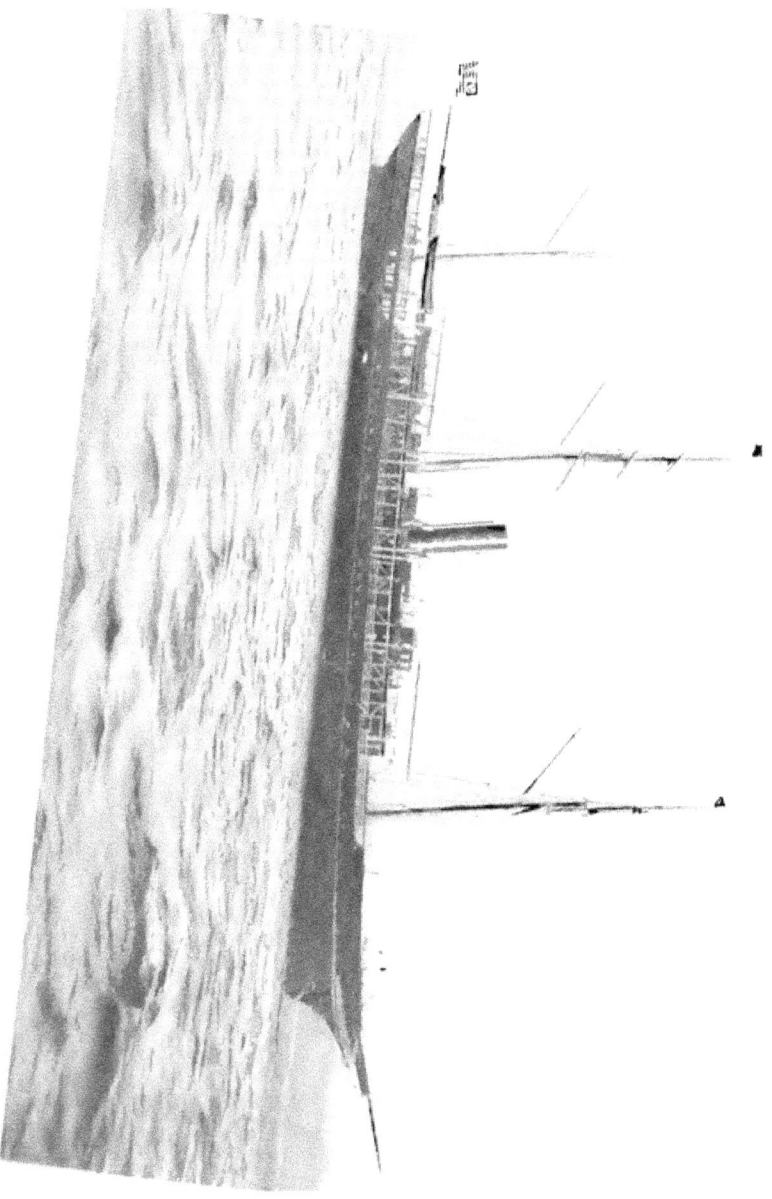

THE NIAGARA'S FIGUREHEAD

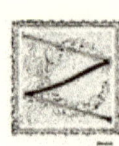

NIAGARA'S figure-head is a skilfully carved representation of an American eagle, with wings outstretched, gilded with gold leaf, and bearing upon its breast a United States shield in colors. In its talons are a number of Indian arrows. The figure is large and life-like in appearance. The ornamental work of the prow is touched out with gold.

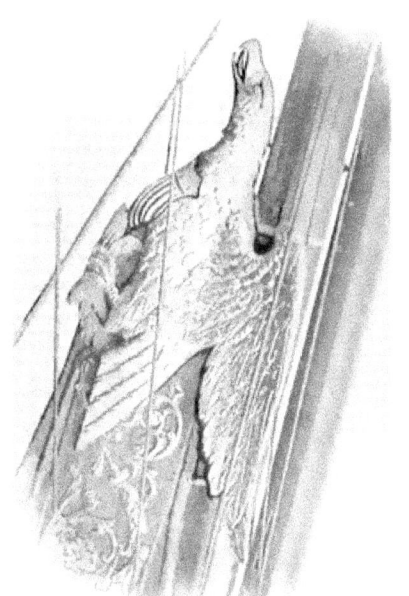

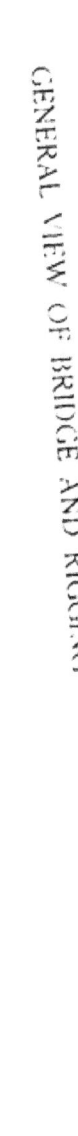

GENERAL VIEW OF BRIDGE AND RIGGING

N the spar deck, the house, which is built of steel and covered with mahogany, is 110 feet long and 10 feet wide. Above this, at the forward end and on a level with the bridge, which is furnished with every modern device for signalling to the most distant parts of the ship, is the wheel-house, which will be used in stormy weather. It contains a chart cabinet, an electrical signalling apparatus, and an electrical key-board for operating the steam whistle. On the wall is a dial which shows whether the numerous bulkhead doors are closed. The yacht can be steered by steam, electricity, or by hand.

The boat equipment of the Niagara includes a 35-foot steam launch capable of a speed of 10½ miles an hour; a 24-foot naphtha launch, two 25-foot lifeboats, a 22-foot gig, an 18-foot market boat, and two dingeys. The yacht will also carry, in the near future, the fastest one-rater that can be built. Whenever desirable the boat will be entered in regattas. Mr. Gould's purpose being to stimulate and encourage the building and sailing of small yachts.

THE PROMENADE DECK

The upper deck offers an unbroken promenade the full length of the ship, an advantage which few ocean-going yachts possess. During the summer the entire deck will be protected from the glare of the sun by overhead awnings. Comfortable chairs of artistic pattern are scattered about for the convenience of the owner's guests. Forward under the bridge is located the owner's chart room. In addition to the usual instruments it is equipped with a large globe and a complete nautical library. Just behind the chart room is the commander's quarters. An observation room, half open to the weather, is a feature of the deck-house.

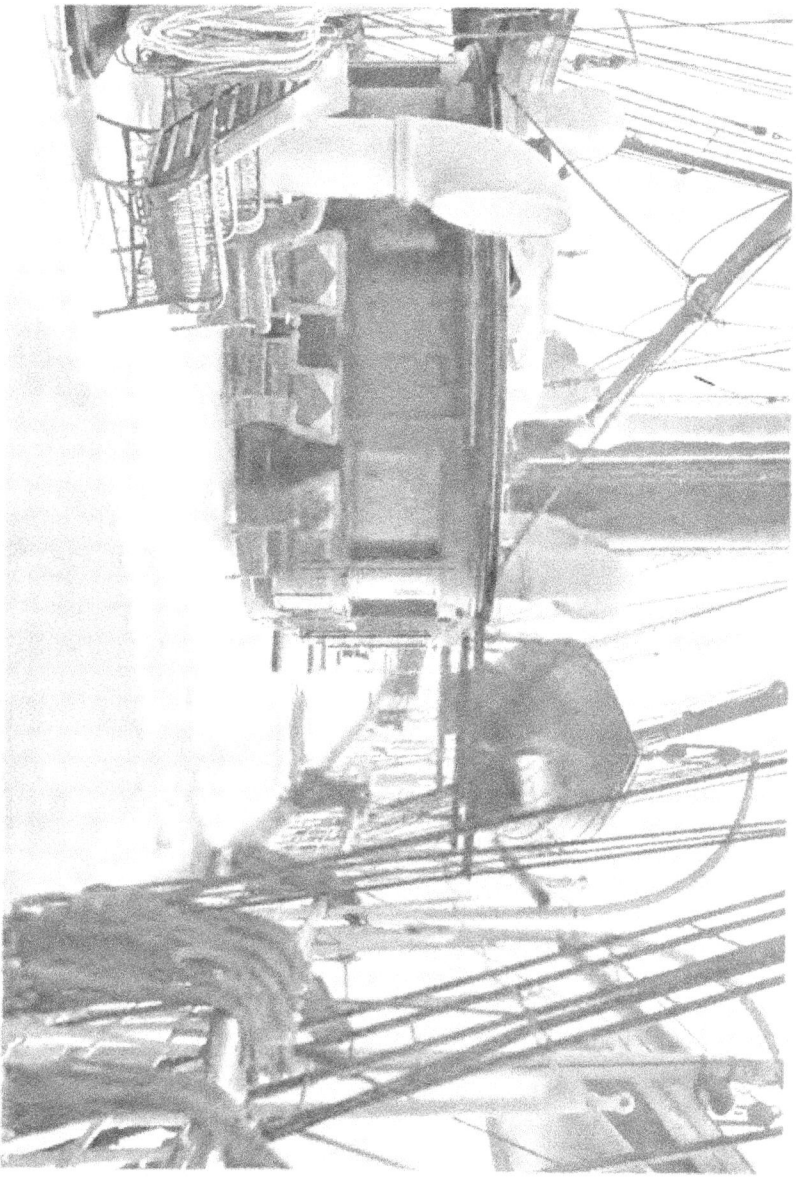

OWNER'S OFFICE ON PROMENADE DECK

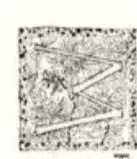

R. Gould's office on the promenade deck is located just beyond the smoking-room. It is finished in East Indian mahogany, the carpet and damask curtains being of a rich dark green. It contains a large mahogany desk, a typewriter cabinet of the same material, an inviting divan covered with velvet cushions which can be used as a bed, several reclining and easy-chairs, and a table. Sconces with opalescent green shades above the owner's desk complete the decorations of the room. Several large windows on each side of the room furnish an abundance of daylight. The office is easy of access from the card-room or music hall by a narrow passage, thus obviating the necessity of going out on deck during rough or stormy weather.

MUSIC HALL ON PROMENADE DECK
TWO VIEWS

OR the comfort of his guests the owner has provided a number of special rooms. The largest of these is the music hall on the upper deck, 16 feet wide and 32 feet long, finished in African mahogany and upholstered in dark green. Wide windows, consisting of single panes of heavy plate glass, give plenty of light and afford an excellent opportunity for observation in rainy weather. A concert orchestrion, equivalent to a band of eighteen pieces, furnishes music for dancing or plays the latest songs and instrumental compositions whenever desired. Hanging on the wall at one end of the hall is a Sixteenth-century tapestry picture representing a village dance.

Two ornamental stained glass skylights in the ceiling add to the room's attractiveness and assist in its proper ventilation.

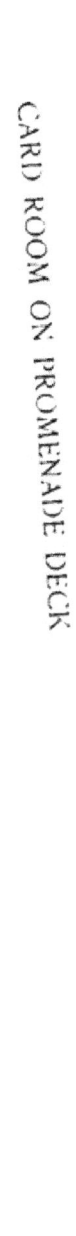

CARD ROOM ON PROMENADE DECK

JUST beyond the music hall is the card-room, in old oak, furnished with big easy-chairs and comfortable lounging divans covered with soft Venetian leather. A heavy oaken sideboard, with the usual accessories, occupies one corner of the room. In one end is concealed a dumb-waiter which communicates with the steward's pantry on the main deck. The combination card-tables are so arranged that almost any kind of a parlor game can be played upon them. The walls are decorated with old Dutch delft plaques, the globes over the electric lights being of a design that harmonizes with them.

LIBRARY AND STAIRCASE

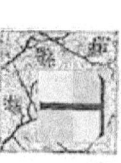

The library, on the main deck, is approached from the dining-saloon by a wide archway, and from the music hall on the deck above by a broad stairway, the balustrade of which is one of the best examples of black walnut carving produced in '98. The latter is composed of a series of massive wreaths joined at the top by graceful garlands. The newel post supports an artistic group of bronze cupids who hold aloft floral branches in which glow-lamps burn. The library is finished in American black walnut with hangings of Venetian red. Around the walls stand bookcases filled with over 600 volumes of novels, biographies, travels, etc., suited to every taste. At one end are two covered glass cases containing a carefully-selected assortment of arms, such as revolvers, cutlasses, rifles, and swords. A writing desk, a wall cabinet for bric-a-brac, a broad leather-covered seat, and some easy reading-chairs complete the furnishings of the room.

MRS. GOULD'S SUITE
a.—GENERAL VIEW
b.—BEDROOM

SEVERAL novel features are presented in the interior of the yacht, which was planned by Mrs. Gould herself. The owner's and guests' living apartments are as absolutely private as they are in a town house. They are completely cut off from those occupied by the crew, and cannot be visited except under orders. This arrangement assures the greatest privacy, and many of the annoyances which have hitherto prevailed on steam yachts may thus be avoided. One thing which has contributed to this desirable end is the elimination of the conventional and universally prevalent grand staircase leading from the dining-saloon to the upper deck. All of this space has been utilized in adding to the size of the dining-saloon on the main deck and to the social hall on the spar deck.

Mrs. Gould's suite, located on the port side of the main deck, consists of boudoir, bedroom, dressing-room, and bath, in ivory and rose of the Louis XVI. period.

The draperies about the portholes, the royal canopy of rich silk above the couch of spotless white, and the velvet carpet upon the floor, are of a delicate shade of rose, in which garlands and bows of ribbon are worked in graceful design.

The dressing-room is brilliantly illuminated from the ceiling by glow-lamps set in tulip-shaped opalescent glass shades. A large, full-length, three-leaved folding mirror is one of the features of this room.

BOUDOIR IN MRS. GOULD'S SUITE

LEADING from the bedroom is a private hall connecting with the boudoir, which corresponds to the dressing-room in general tone effect. The globes of the electric lamps are half-open roses of opalescent glass. Wall cabinets of French plate glass; a beautiful writing desk of the Louis XIV. period; a long, low divan piled high with silken cushions, and, above it, an Oriental canopy, from which hangs a colored glass lantern of novel design, are among the attractions of the apartment. A bathroom in ivory and rose tiles, fitted with electric tub and foot baths, completes the suite.

MR. GOULD'S SUITE

R. GOULD'S suite, which adjoins that of his wife, consists of three commodious rooms, on the starboard side of the yacht, finished in natural birch, the carpet and draperies being of Yale blue. The largest contains a brass bedstead, a roll-top desk, and a safe. A telephone stands at the head of the bed, by means of which the owner can communicate with all parts of the ship.

The dressing-room is furnished with a bureau, a mirror, closets for clothes, and the usual accessories. From this suite doors lead to Mrs. Gould's suite, the dining-room, and a hall from which a staircase leads to the upper deck.

MR. GOULD'S bathroom is one of the most complete ever placed on board a yacht. It is a large, well-ventilated apartment, the walls and floor being covered with white tiles, having a blue flower in the centre. It is fitted with shower, tub, and foot baths, and is heated in cool weather by electricity. Much attention has been paid to the plumbing, not only of this room, but of all the rooms of similar character on the yacht. The floors are first covered with sheet-lead on which the tiles are then laid in cement. This arrangement prevents any possibility of leakage in case water should be accidently spilled.

DINING-ROOM ON THE MAIN DECK

A.— ONYX FIREPLACE
B.— PIANO IN A CARVED OAK CASE

N board the Niagara, the dining-saloon is the largest room, its dimensions being 36 x 24 feet. It is finished in hand-carved quartered oak and decorated with old Renaissance tapestry. At one end is a serviceable open fireplace enclosed with slabs of delicately tinted Mexican onyx, above which rises an elaborately carved mantel of oak bearing in bold relief a representation of Diana standing, spear in hand, ready for the chase. Directly opposite the fireplace rests an upright piano in a massively carved oak case which matches the rest of the apartment. Three old tapestry panels in the top complete its decorations.

The high-backed chairs belonging to this room are also made of carved oak upholstered with tapestry. On four sideboards of stout oak curiously carved are displayed the owner's elaborate dinner service in gold and silver. Ten large porthole windows and two skylights of tinted glass flood the saloon with sunlight during the day, and at night scores of electric bulbs half-hidden in the ceiling diffuse a soft mellow glow over the apartment.

THE STEWARD'S PANTRY

 BEYOND the dining-room is the steward's pantry, which is much larger than those usually found in pretentious city houses. It is furnished with several china closets with glass fronts, and racks in the ceiling which hold the goblets, wine glasses, etc. Ice boxes for the storage of wines, fruits, butter and vegetables for immediate use are conveniently located. The wood-work is light in color, and the walls are covered with white tiles. An abundance of light is obtained from several large port-holes. Every possible convenience is provided for cleaning the silver and glass-ware.

GENERAL VIEW OF OWNER'S KITCHEN

CONNECTING directly with the pantry is the kitchen or galley, Mr. Gould's chef having a range for his special use. The walls of the kitchen are covered with white enamelled tiles and the floor with serviceable vitreous brick arranged in appropriate designs. It is fitted with every modern appliance for the prompt preparation and speedy service of meals, including an electric range and heater. The chef who cooks for the crew has a separate kitchen service. A bake-shop, equipped with the usual appliances for turning out a daily supply of bread for the owner's guests and the crew of the yacht, is a feature of this department.

STAIRCASE IN LOWER HALL.

FORWARD of Mr. and Mrs. Gould's suites, on the main deck, are four guest chambers opening from a broad, richly carpeted hall. They are 12 feet square and each is finished in a different kind of wood, the beauty of the grain of each being carefully brought out by hand polishing. The carpets and the hangings match the color of the woodwork. One of the chambers is in curly maple, another in sycamore, the third in prima vera, and the fourth in California redwood. On the lower deck, reached by a broad staircase, are three more guest chambers of the same character, though finished in different woods, and like them provided with private bath-rooms, the tiling of which has a dash of color to match. Each is furnished with a brass bed, a bureau with a large plate-glass mirror, a wall writing-desk, and a cedar-lined clothes closet.

In addition to those already enumerated there are rooms for Mr. Gould's private secretary, doctor, valet, and personal servants; an apothecary shop, a photographer's room, a fully equipped steam laundry, a hospital, and a room for fishing tackle and camping outfit.

THE CREW'S QUARTERS.

The space devoted to the comfort of the crew is a striking feature of the NIAGARA. One of the first orders given by Mr. Gould, when the construction of the yacht was begun, was that the men who were to run the engines, fire the boilers, and take care of the ship should have attractive living rooms.

As a result of the provisions made the NIAGARA's crew of 78 men have the most commodious quarters to be found on any yacht. The forecastle is a large, well-lighted, and well-ventilated room painted white. The bunks are constructed of light iron framework, with wide spaces between each tier, and are furnished with an abundance of blankets and comfortables. The officers occupy state-rooms which compare favorably with those found on ocean steamships.

Aft on the main deck is a recreation hall for the men. It extends the entire width of the ship, the sea walls being so arranged that they can be opened when desired, thus giving the crew what is practically an open deck.

THE ELECTRIC PLANT.

The electric-light plant consists of two direct-connected dynamos and engines installed in duplicate, each set having a capacity of 400 16-candle-power lamps. There is a storage battery of 80 lights capacity installed in a convenient place and wired up complete. The direct-connected four-pole multipolar generators are driven by a 6 x 5 double-enclosed Sturtevant engine, running at a speed of 550 revolutions per minute under a boiler pressure of 100 lbs., which will develop 40 horse-power. There is also one polished brass type "D" Rushmore pilot-house projector, 18 inches in diameter, taking 45 amperes, the whole wired and installed complete.

The wiring of the ship was done by the electrical staff of the builders, and the whole installation was finished complete by their workmen. The various outlets are arranged on six circuits, and the installation and wiring are done in the most approved manner, with all provisions possible for safety and artistic effect. The plant is provided with the usual instruments and spares for operation at sea.

On nights when an illumination is desired two lights outlining the hull, masts, and spars of the yacht can be used at one time in addition to the great searchlight on the bridge.

The part which electricity plays upon this palatial craft is a most important one. It runs the big orchestrion in the music hall, cooks steaks in the kitchen, warms the rooms, lights cigars, operates the laundry machinery, heats my lady's curling tongs, carries messages over the telephone wires, summons the servants, and cools the air with whirling fans.

THE NIAGARA'S ENGINES.

The engines of the NIAGARA are of the triple-expansion, inverted cylinder, direct-acting, surface-condensing type, with a working pressure of 160 pounds to the square inch. The cylinders are 18, 28, and 45 inches respectively, with a 30-inch stroke. The steam is supplied by three Scotch boilers, each having three furnaces. There are two sets of engines, so that in case one set becomes disabled the yacht can still proceed under the other. The coal bunkers have a capacity of 450 tons, a quantity sufficient to take the NIAGARA to Southampton and back at a twelve-knot speed. The contract speed of the boat is fourteen knots an hour. She is classed under the highest classification at English Lloyds and United States standard, being for a twenty-year rating under special survey.

The yacht is completely fitted with handling gear, including steam capstan and steam windlass forward, and independent steam capstan aft, together with a special steam winch on forecastle for quick-handling purposes, and a steam engine with two gypsies located amidships for the sole purpose of hoisting the steam launches and small boats. There is also a hand-screw gear aft for relief-steering purposes.

THE REFRIGERATING PLANT.

The refrigerating plant is a Remington No. 2 machine, with a capacity of four hundred pounds of ice per day, and to cool fifteen hundred cubic feet of space to a temperature of 34° F. The machine has two

4 x 9-inch vertical single-acting ammonia cylinders on one housing, operated by a 7 x 7-inch vertical engine direct-connected on the same base, complete with all attachments. There is also one ammonia condenser of the submerged type, consisting of a salt-water tank with ammonia-liquifying coils of extra heavy pipe, with all valves and connections.

There is one steel brine tank five feet four inches long by two feet eight inches wide and thirty-six inches deep, with removable covers, provided with necessary ammonia expansion coils of extra heavy pipe, with all valves and connections, arranged to contain fifteen galvanized ice cans, with covers, to hold fifty-pound cakes of ice; and one 3 x 2 x 3-inch duplex steam pump, brass mounted, for brine circulation, with brine gauge, lubricator, and brass-cased thermometer complete. A system of galvanized piping is erected in the cold-storage room and refrigerators for the circulation of the brine. There are two ammonia gauges mounted on an ornamental board, and one ammonia receiver, and connecting pipes, valves, and fittings for the system.

In connection with the machinery department there is an evaporating and distilling plant of fifteen tons capacity.

WATER SUPPLY AND DRAINAGE SYSTEM.

Abundant provisions have been made for furnishing the owner, his guests, and crew with fresh water. Tanks having a capacity of over 15,000 gallons are conveniently located for this purpose.

Much attention has been given by the builders of the Niagara to the subject of drainage. A double service of pipes is provided, one connecting all of the basins and tubs in the owner's quarters with a five hundred gallon tank in the hold, and the other connecting the bathrooms and water-closets with sewage tanks similarly located. The contents of these tanks are pumped overboard by steam or water siphon.

www.ingramcontent.com/pod-product-compliance
Lightning Source LLC
Chambersburg PA
CBHW020325090426
42735CB00009B/1414